I AM THAT I AM

[Exodus 3:14 KJV]

Copyright © Lisa Eva Maria

Acknowledgements

For her unwavering love and faith in me, I thank the Divine Mother who carried me through my darkest hours in the comforting and sacred way she does. And to my daughter Mia Krystina, I adore you and thank you for activating my awakening.

———

An introduction

from the Author

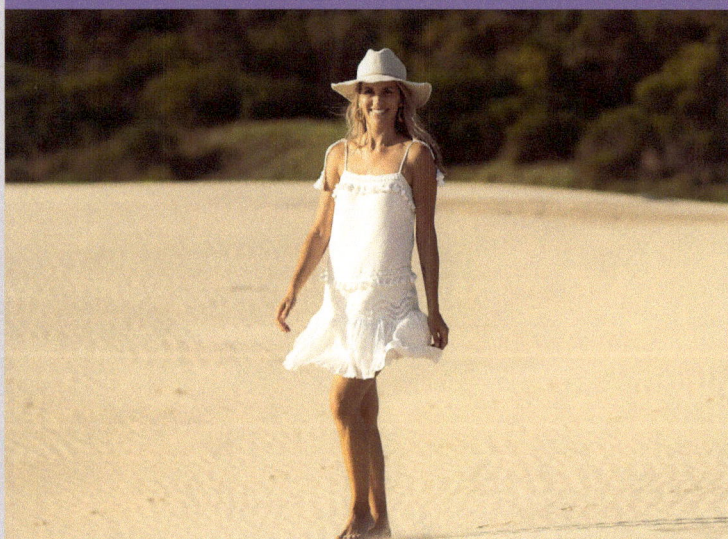

In 2022 before this book came to be, I was sitting in the middle of my living room with a pen and paper and began to write the words I AM THAT I AM repeatedly until it covered the page. I didn't pause to question it or discover what it meant, I simply felt compelled to write and so I did. I experienced a state of complete presence like nothing else existed, but the resonance of these words.

I'd always enjoyed writing, but something shifted after this experience, and I'd engage more frequently with the practice of intuitive writing. Words seemed to be placed in my consciousness, bypassing the intellect. There was no thought process involved, and I couldn't hear words audibly, the best way to describe it is a stream of consciousness downloading words to form a message. The messages were insightful and most helpful, but it was the energy behind the words which felt healing and compassionate in all instances.

I was experiencing a greater level of awakening which seemed to be accelerated after I left Sydney Australia in December 2020, seeking solace in regional New South Wales when the world was getting flipped on its head in response to a pandemic. But as many seekers discover, awakening is a gruelling and inescapable process in which the mind, body and soul undergo a metamorphosis, just like a butterfly. This new environment became my cocoon, an incubation space to clear the old beliefs trapped on the deepest levels of my psyche so I can learn to see, hear and know myself and the world around me on a deeper level. One day my main spirit guide told me, "everything is about to change" and I grieved while not feeling his presence, but in his seeming absence is when I devoted more faith in communion with God and intuitive writing.

I often wondered where the messages were coming from. Was it my higher self, my innate wisdom communicating? I decided I didn't need to know, it wasn't important. I'd just receive them graciously.

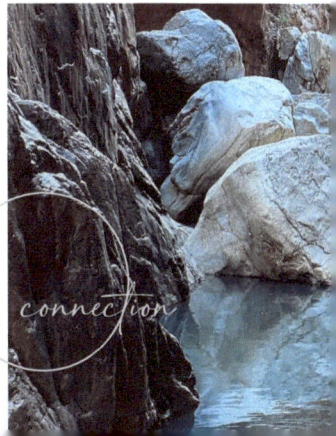

connection

The following year I felt inspired to travel solo to central Australia, a place I hadn't been and never felt the urge to visit. I didn't realise until after booking the flights and accommodation that I'd be embarking on the seventh day of the seventh month of a seven year (7-7-2023), and I don't believe in coincidences. I'm a life path seven, seven is a sacred number and Uluru is known to be a sacred site. Evidently I was embarking on a spirit journey of some kind, but I boarded the flight with no expectations. My intention was to simply enjoy the adventure and bring my laptop along to also spend time working on a writing project I felt committed to.

I departed the flight in Alice Springs and explored the West McDonnell Ranges, a majestic natural landscape deeply rich in cultural significance for its traditional owners, the Arrernte people. The spirit of the land captivated me, I'd fall to my knees in reverence and appreciation for the way she danced with me, magnifying my own spirit and radiance.

For most of the trip I'd rise well before sunrise to write, then explore, walk and *be with country* for most of the day and spend most evenings writing or researching. Every resource I turned to Ascended Master Saint Germain was making himself known to me. I began researching him and there was no doubt in my heart I was in his presence. I'd ask myself questions to help gain clarity for my writing project and Saint Germain seemed to be answering through these other sources.

I travelled down to Yulara by coach and spent one morning on a sunrise trek around Uluru. It was a cold morning, and I rugged up with many layers and commenced walking with the group, but eventually went off on my own at a preferred pace. Observing the rise of a new dawn upon the horizon in the outback is quite spectacular. I was mesmerised by the morning sun lighting up this sacred site, drinking it in through my senses.

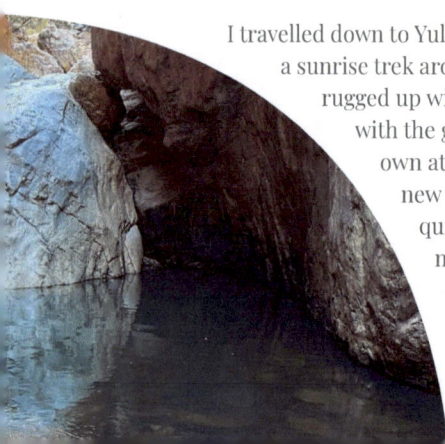

The natural surrounds felt surreal, like witnessing a scene from a movie set and I'd observe in awe and wonder, is any of it real? Much of it looked like props; all perfect, but so alive! The warmth of the sun, the breeze dancing with the trees and the pristine waters, the wild and colourful desert flowers and the rich red soil. When I think about the landscape, I can still feel the spirit of it dancing through every cell of my body.

That afternoon I sat on the bed with my laptop in the hotel room watching Uluru at a distance. My ongoing curiosity for Saint Germain led me to continue more research about him and when I discovered a woman who is a trance channel for Saint Germain based in America, his presence filled the room, an energy so expansive, so powerful it was electrifying! I felt it through my body, an activation was taking place and I burst into tears, the energy was overwhelming, extraordinary and larger than life! It subsided moments later, but the aftereffects were apparent. I could feel my cells buzzing with new life and I knew I had to contact this woman.

I arranged a session with her and Saint Germain for when I returned home. As I was preparing myself for the session I heard the words telepathically: "It is safe for you to be powerful." I knew it was Saint Germain.

I was ready.

I spent twelve months developing a direct relationship with Saint Germain as a trusted teacher and source of support. He introduced me to the Violet Flame and his teachings were centered on reconnecting with my inner power, freedom and mastery. The human experience is no walk in the park, but the tools and knowledge available to us at this unprecedented time on Earth are more accessible than ever and the resources and abilities we carry within us are ready and waiting to be activated.

The messages throughout this book are predominately direct from Saint Germain. He has quite a playful, jovial energy. Initially it was experienced as separate from me, but over time I've learnt to become the energy I'm channelling as it feels more effective and authentic. You'll notice occasional references to 'we' which relates to other Ascended Masters associated with Saint Germain's network including the late Elizabeth Clare Prophet, fondly known as "Guru Ma", who provided the message titled 'All Have The Opportunity To Ascend'.

The Ascended Masters are like loving brothers and sisters who are here to help us. They know what it's like to walk this Earth realm and their messages are a loving and uplifting source of encouragement.

May the words within this book activate a remembrance of your own inner power to shine and serve the light of your heart.

With Love

Lisa Eva Maria

There lies a great power within you which can only be accessed by living with a higher state of consciousness.

POWER IS HERE FOR YOU NOW

Greetings dear one. Power is here for you now. The great unseen is present for every one of you upon planet Earth to help steer the ship in a NEW direction. We await your call for assistance, and we ask you to trust – to believe it to be true and it will be so.

Arise at dawn and come into the stillness of the early morning. Visualise and feel the warmth of the sun's rays shine a light upon your great being and know that you are on path. Breathe in the abundance of possibilities available for you NOW and lean into the quiet whispers of your heart. Therein lies a great many treasures and your connection with the most high Source for you are not separate from this Source.

You must come to understand there lies a great power within you which can only be accessed by living with a higher state of consciousness. So, every time you experience suffering – do not deny the experience. We ask that you acknowledge it and fill it with LOVE. Call upon us to assist in the transmutation of the density and it will be done.

Faith is your ally.

August, 2023

Arise into the greatness that you are
with a little more tenderness and praise
for your efforts to lean into love
and wondrous possibilities.

A GREATER PLAN IS UNFOLDING

There is a stirring in your heart which knows a greater plan is unfolding and there is much confusion and distress on the planet for it's the direct result of the inner turmoil as one shifts and sorts through their subconscious and attempts to realise all the aspects of self inhibiting higher ways of living and being in greater harmony with self and the other.

Great compassion for self is needed at this time as you come to understand there is more to life on Earth than you have been told and if one is not willing to listen to the voice of the higher self, attuned to a deeper knowing beyond the physical eye, it becomes increasingly difficult to make sense of the madness dominating the minds of many at this time.

Arise dear one! Arise into the greatness that you are with a little more tenderness and praise for your efforts to lean into love and wondrous possibilities.

August, 2023

*Lean into your sense of curiosity and you
will discover deeper aspects of yourself
willing and ready to be brought forth
for healing or expression.*

THERE ARE A GREAT
MANY HERE TO ASSIST

We are at a pivotal time on this planet unlike anything humanity has ever experienced. No matter how many times you have returned here, it has never been quite the same as what is being experienced now. There are a great many here to assist the evolution of the collective consciousness of humanity. It is imperative that one attempts to awaken all aspects of self in need of love.

It's a time of letting go, of stripping back the layers and trauma everyone carries within them, for all are from the ONE collective consciousness and it's your responsibility to learn to see through the eyes and heart of love and feel with a loving and compassionate heart.

So, there are many teachers brought forth at this time in physical form, but we ask you allow the evolution of your own consciousness to guide you to the most suitable support for you. There is no wrong way. Allow yourself to FEEL and experience a resonance before accepting information or knowledge as truth. Lean into your sense of curiosity and you will discover deeper aspects of yourself willing and ready to be brought forth for healing or expression.

August, 2023

To simplify, one must be willing to declutter the environment and the mind.

SIMPLIFY YOUR APPROACH

Relinquish the burdens through simplicity. To simplify, one must be willing to declutter the environment and the mind.

As you eliminate that which you don't need, you create space for BEing and allowing Creation to move through you. What can you do today to start eliminating that which is clogging you up from being a clear conduit for co-creation?

This month clear the space; the home, car, devices, wardrobe, from anything taking up unnecessary space. Simplify your approach to personal admin and other affairs. Clean out the junk restricting FLOW.

Free yourself to enable simplicity and ease to prevail.

September, 2023

Breathe in the goodness of that which you are.

BREATHE IN THE GOODNESS

Treat yourself with utmost care as there is more destined for your path which will see you rising into a fuller expression of who you are and what you came to fulfil at this time. There is no greater place to be than right where you are, expanding your heart in each moment.

Breathe in the goodness of that which you are, for it is all here for you now. Allow yourself to be IN-appreciation throughout the day to enable even greater experiences to arise for you.

The sun shines forth at this time to illuminate the collective awakening of the soul of humanity.

There is no need to seek for it is all within you. Lean into that which you are in this NOW moment and rejoice in your power, beauty and creative force.

Let love be your guide.

September, 2023

*The ripple effect of your higher vibrations
have positive effects, reaching far and wide.*

YOUR TRUE NORTH

This great awakening taking place sheds light on aspects of your soul ready to shine. This is an exciting time because it allows you to SEE what was unseen and KNOW what was unknown. Through this awareness, you are better informed to steer yourself in the direction of most importance to your heart - your True North - the path which will see you elevating your frequency and radiating this into the world.

The ripple effect of your higher vibrations have positive effects, reaching far and wide. It is wise to focus on your own lane. By doing so, you're also impacting the world at large.

Do what you can in alignment with your True North and great wonders await!

September, 2023

Be the love that you are and willing
to see things from a higher perspective
and peace shall reign again.

SEE THINGS FROM A HIGHER PERSPECTIVE

Love is here for all to experience, yet many remain in fear of the greatest potential for healing and JOY on this planet.

Since all is of the MIND, everyone can rewire their thought processes in order to see things from a higher perspective, quite like the Eagle which soars at great heights.

But are you willing?

For without the will to broaden your horizons, your perspective remains limited and consequently your experience of reality is limited. For this reason, many people are unable to recognise greater Truths.

All souls are on their own unique path of evolution and so is the planet. Experience of life on Earth is moving into a new trajectory and WE are delighted to announce that all is in perfect order.

BE the love that you are and willing to see things from a higher perspective and PEACE shall reign again.

September, 2023

*The choices you make determine
what that seed becomes.*

THE BECOMING

There holds a glorious seed of possibility in the heart of everyone here on the planet. The seed is a spark of potentiality for your path.

The choices you make determine what that seed becomes. In order for it to become or evolve into its purest potential, it requires nourishment. For this reason, reflect on ways you are not nourishing the self: mind, body and spirit as one whole form.

It's no coincidence early on your path you discover the importance of self-care, for it supports the foundation; the strength and health of the seed, to grow into its destined form.

There is a need to consider all the ways you are not nourishing yourself and how you can reshape your choices to nourish your seed of potential.

October, 2023

Affirm: I AM THAT I AM

YOUR MIGHTY I AM PRESENCE IS UNSHAKEABLE

An invitation to call forth your Mighty I AM Presence in this time of challenge. There is much deception stirring on the planet as forces are desperate to hold on to their need for power and control.

But your mighty I AM Presence is unshakeable.

Since there is no separation from the ultimate Source, there is always the ability to BE the mighty I AM Presence that you are.

The battle is only in the mind and as you learn to master this, you claim your dominion and miracles are inevitable. You are the miracle, you simply have forgotten. So as you awaken your I AM Presence, you are claiming your birthright; to be free and live resourced with all the abundance necessary to walk your path unencumbered.

For you are deeply loved.

October, 2023

*Alignment is key to stepping
into your power.*

ALIGNMENT

The battle is awake in all as you move into a deeper understanding of what is present at this time and acceptance is no easy task. For with acceptance you are handed responsibility for your next steps. It can be too much for some. But for those who accept the mission to align with what sets their heart on fire, in service to the most high Source, will be resourced.

Alignment is key to stepping into your power. For when your actions align with the stirrings of your heart, an alchemic reaction takes place, and everything aspires to make it so.

Go forth without conviction – but in presence – surrendering to what you know in your heart is possible.

October, 2023

Forgiveness lights the way to a brand new day and illuminates the essence of who you are.

FORGIVENESS LIGHTS THE WAY

The storms will pass for those allowing forgiveness to take place. A great humbling occurs when you forgive and let go of all aspects within you and people around you which have escalated the suffering. All have been great teachings/ teachers. And as you recognise the lessons, it is easier to forgive.

There is power in REBIRTH when you don't carry with you the heavy load of days gone by; resentment, heartache, disappointment.

Forgiveness is a vital part in letting go; forgiving yourself for unloving choices you've made and forgiving others for their unloving behaviours.

Forgiveness lights the way to a brand new day and illuminates the essence of who you are. It ignites the flame in your heart for unconditional love to prevail and transmutes suffering on the planet.

October, 2023

There is so much beauty in the present moment and this expands as you appreciate it.

THE NEED FOR PRESENCE

Don't let times of great uncertainty overshadow the need for presence.
The more you focus on the future, you miss the experience of what is
here for you now. For there is so much beauty in the present moment
and this expands as you appreciate it.

Your breath, witnessing the smile of a child, watching the branches
dance in the breeze.

BEing in the here and now determines the next moment for it is
simply a sequence of moments creating an experience.

Delight in your vision, dreams and aspirations but always return to
the NOW and rejoice in the beauty you find there.

October, 2023

Be the observer of your inner dialogue and ask yourself, how is this making me feel?

YOUR INNER DIALOGUE

Let love lead the way. Let love lead the way.

We repeat this message as a reminder to release anything unloving from your thoughts for there is great JOY to be experienced yet many stay trapped in the confinement of displeasing thoughts. The more one focuses on this, the more one escalates the drama in their own consciousness and it plays out in their reality.

Listen and See what is there to witness, but nothing is more important to witness than that which is going on in your MIND.

Be the observer of your inner dialogue and ask yourself, how is this making me feel? For your world and experience will become an energetic match to the vibration emanating from your inner dialogue.

Be kind to yourself and the world around you for this practice fosters great healing within the realm of your perceived reality and beyond.

You are deeply loved.

November, 2023

Take the next step forward in faith,
surrendering to the dance
which follows.

TAKE THE NEXT STEP FORWARD

Wait for no-one and no-thing to embark on what's alive in your heart. Your freedom lies in giving yourself permission to take the next step forward in faith, surrendering to the dance which follows. Doors will open into realms which delight and destined connections are awaiting close by.

In sweet time you will realise that keeping the faith despite influencing energies attempting to pull you in other directions will see you align with the GIFT already waiting for you. It's calling on courage to take that leap.

So look up, around
And tell me what you see
For this is a realm of possibility.
Great wonders await
For those who have faith
We wish you'd give way
To the trumpets that play,
Singing in a New Dream.

November, 2023

Courageously surrender to the rhythm
equipped with your unique resources.

COURAGE

You are stepping into a fuller expression of yourself and the COURAGE to shine a light on that which you are has had many opportunities for practice.

The courage to shed limiting beliefs. The courage to embody your values. The courage to express what's True in your heart.

Frequent acts of courage, despite the presence of fear, builds strength to breakdown barriers preventing you from claiming your birth right and sing it out loud.

Don't just think it - BE it.

You have been blinded, unable to recognise your power, wisdom and resources you carry within you from lifetimes of experiences here. Many even undermine their abilities to not 'ruffle anyone's feathers'. Enough of that!

The resources within you are there for a reason and as you honour it, you activate everything you need. So courageously surrender to the rhythm, equipped with your unique resources to help you learn to dance with the Divine.

November, 2023

Anything unloving is simply an illusion.

ILLUSIONS

Expect all to unfold before your eyes for everything your heart desires is within reach. Love always finds a way to make right the injustices of one's experiences when one remains in alignment with the path of love.

Anything unloving is simply an illusion made holy for the sake of mankind to witness the impact of frequencies less than Christ perfection.

Can you feel what's possible unfolding within your being? The rise above the density is happening NOW as the collective rises in consciousness to bring forth a new era destined for Earth and her beloved HUmans.

You ALL truly are children of God ~ ALL perfection ~ ONE Universal Consciousness giving form through diverse expressions.

Rejoice and let love lead the way.

November, 2023

Nothing is impossible.

BELIEVE

A troubled heart is one which loses FAITH in LOVE and all things possible.

Do not doubt what's possible for this creates a wall from an experience which lingers in the field but has not quite manifest ... you must BELIEVE.

How many miracles must you witness before accepting this to be so?

Faith keeps the heart strong and sets the mind free of troubles. While some days your faith will waver and doubt sets in, know such days present an opportunity to rekindle your faith. Close your eyes and believe, for nothing is impossible. Use your imagination and breathe.

December, 2023

Pay attention to the signs and synchronicities.

SIGNS & SYNCHRONICITIES

Delight in the signs and synchronicities. Pay attention to them for they help you witness the magic that's possible and show you the dance with the Divine.

Celebrate the dance; celebrate the signs and synchronicities and witness the wonder and beauty on the path you walk.

Signs and synchronicities light the compass of your heart to help navigate your way. As you appreciate this direct guidance, the clearer and more trusting you will become. Have faith in your footsteps. There is no wrong way, only detours to what's possible and discoveries toward all you came to BE.

December, 2023

*Remain focused on the goodness
of your experience.*

SING IT FROM THE ROOFTOPS

Fear not, the battle has come undone as many step into a realm of vast expansion. The glitter of hope was the tone of yesterday, the power of love is the solution and is rising in the field of human consciousness.

Arise and breathe in the freshness of new beginnings. A season unlike anything before, for many are leading the way to a greater world through their presence and state of consciousness - being a Golden Ray - demonstrating what's possible despite turmoil also playing out; the repercussions of insanity.

Remain focussed on the goodness of your experience. Sing it from the rooftops, show others what's possible when you lead with your heart and embody your I AM presence.

December, 2023

It's the ripple effect of small victories which create a force field of celebration.

CREATE A FORCE FIELD
OF CELEBRATION

Open, receptive, free. Be that.

A world unlike anyone has ever experienced awaits. While great change in imminent, know that so too are great possibilities and recognising one's power to transmute all suffering.

As more and more people begin to step away from the will of the ego and into the will of one's sacred heart the outcome is obvious, is it not?

It truly is a delight to watch the transmutation take place within oneself and the collective. For a greater plan is at work and the glory of God is rising.

Celebrate the victories, for no victory is too small. It's the ripple effect of small victories which create a force field of celebration - joy, laughter and wonder in the realm of creation and possibilities that you reside.

It truly is a gift to be on Earth at this time.

———————————

December, 2023

Enjoy the empty cup and it shall be filled
with inspiration to light up your heart.

AN EMPTY CUP

An empty cup may seem like it has nothing to give, but this is not true. An empty cup is of great value because it has the space to be put to use when the time is ripe.

For those of you who feel their cup is empty at this time, allow it to be this way. There is no need to go searching to fill the 'emptiness', which some refer to as the 'void', for it truly is a gift.

When you come to accept the empty cup and appreciate the space you've cultivated within to rest and delight in the here and now, that's when divine intelligence weaves its way through inspiration.

Enjoy the empty cup and it shall be filled with inspiration to light up your heart.

January, 2024

Call upon the violet flame to assist the transmutation and it shall be done.

CALL UPON THE VIOLET FLAME

Let it be done by the violet flame, a vibration which transmutes all suffering. Shower yourself in violet frequencies to purify the energies out of alignment with your higher self, obstructing the flow of greater ease and grace.

This frequency holds great power for those who call upon the violet flame and make it a daily ritual; a purification of sorts to help see you through the year ahead.

The power is yours and it requires commitment to self - your higher self - from which pure intentions are made manifest.

Call upon the violet flame to assist the transmutation and it shall be done. Your call is answered.

January, 2024

Delight in joy, like children who
play without hesitation.

DELIGHT IN JOY

Delight in joy, like children who play without hesitation for in the realm of delight there are no boundaries or resistance. It's a space to be free and rejoice in all the colours and forms on this Earth.

If you struggle to be like a child from time to time, simply observe a child's desire for freedom; a curiosity and imagination to explore the unknown without fear.

There are indeed many children who have not the experience of such liberties however, as you observe those who do and align with your own playful and curious inner child, you elevate your own frequency and it sends ripples of possibilities for transmutation to take place within the collective toward a world where all children, people and living beings live free to be the fullest expression of the divine spark which resides in ALL.

January, 2024

*Stop thinking your way into creation
and start letting go of all that's inhibiting
alignment with your divine essence.*

YOUR DIRECT LINK TO SOURCE

In the sacred space of your heart is a chamber connecting you to the threefold flame which is your direct link to Source creation. It holds the seed for your presence and purpose on Earth at this time and we ask you to take the time to frequently be still and connect with your heart centre without expectation. Just be in sacred connection and communion with your heart.

Invite the breath into this space and notice your body begin to drop in to reorganise itself to a state of balance and calm. Breathe loving, gentle breaths into this chamber and maintain gentle connection.

This space holds the key to unlock the greatest desires of your heart which is in alignment with the Divine Will - for *God's will* will be done when you get out of your own way and stop thinking your way into creation and start letting go of all that's inhibiting alignment with your divine essence.

From this space creation takes fold and deep fulfilment is made possible.

January, 2024

Your transition is a celebration for the glory of life and the magnificent journey it is.

THE EXPERIENCE YOU WISH TO CREATE

Time is precious on planet Earth for it is limited and should be considered sacred. Whilst many will talk about time being an 'illusion', indeed it is in the grander cosmic realm, but on Earth the concept of 'time' and its associations should be considered more thoughtfully.

For how you spend your time is influencing your limited experience of life on Earth. All time spent is time invested toward the experience you wish to create. If you're not investing your time on experiences which support the lifestyle you desire, then perhaps reorganise your 'time', to make it work for you and not against you.

Far too many get to their last days on Earth feeling regret for what 'could have' been had different choices been made. But it's not too late to make peace with the life which has been lived and appreciate and reflect on the lessons, the gifts and the serendipitous moments which lit up your heart.

'Time is of the essence' as one would say. It's time to reorganise your time to ensure you arrive at your last days rejoicing in the wonder and richness of life on Earth, so your transition is a celebration for the GLORY OF LIFE and the magnificent journey it is.

January, 2024

A true seeker will always discover the golden wisdom within their own heart.

PERSONAL POWER
IS EVER EVOLVING

I speak of wisdom for there are a great many of you who carry much wisdom from lifetimes present on Earth, yet you lean on too strongly to much information outside of you.

Whilst we encourage the 'seeker' to follow the path of their own BEcoming, or perhaps REmembering and the teachers you encounter along the way, a true seeker will always discover the golden wisdom within their own heart.

It's not a time to be giving your power away to others, you've been doing this for too long. It's time to take only what you need and leave the rest. The real glory lies within for how can it not when one honours and nurtures their own direct link to Source.

Personal power is ever evolving within you. Notice the times you give your power away to people and circumstances outside of you and ask, what is this experience teaching me about myself? Notice any dissonance and rejoice in the lessons that make your heart soar with appreciation. For these moments reflect back to you the light and wisdom within.

February, 2024

*The higher self wants you to feel alignment
with higher frequencies.*

IT DOES NOT HELP
TO PITY OTHERS

All beings on Earth are perfectly positioned where they need to be. Many dwell in pity for those in less fortunate circumstances, but you must be willing to accept that all souls have contributed to their positioning on Earth at this time. It does not help to pity others less fortunate than you, for this feeds on the lower densities so many are working intentionally to release themselves from at this time.

The higher self wants you to FEEL alignment with higher frequencies. From this state the act of co-creating innovative solutions, inspired ways of living, support and new developments can arise with greater ease and can assist those who need help.

The old ways of working harder to achieve more is not in alignment with the trajectory of Earth or your physical body. The Earth lives in perfect harmony - are you willing to learn such ways to enable greater ease?

February, 2024

You are positioned with the freedom to make choices which will elevate your consciousness or lower it.

LOVE AND THE
WONDERS OF LOVE

Love and the wonders of love can be quite illusive to those afraid of their very essence. It takes quite a being to return to love when there is so much hardship and unloving behaviours demonstrated in the world. It's apparent in families, in relationships and in the world at large.

I speak many times of willingness in the creation of one's world. Mankind is free to make their own choices – to play with all the colours and determine for oneself the experience one desires to create in this realm. If one inflicts hurt or pain upon another, the colours present in their aura and one remains in the cycle of miscreation. For all creation misaligned with the highest good for all is indeed keeping one afar from that which one most desires and lowers the frequency present within and around their field, thus attracting more of this in their world. The Law of Attraction does not stand alone though, and there are many influencing factors at play with this law, which has become quite 'mainstream' and misconstrued.

You are positioned with the freedom to make choices which will elevate your consciousness or lower it. You are holding seeds of creation, of possibilities in every moment and how you choose to nurture these seeds will impact your experience and worldview. Many are aware if this and still the majority are making choices from the lower mind, propelling needless cycles of suffering.

There's always a choice. Consider reflecting on the thoughts motivating the choices made and determine if it stems from LOVE or FEAR.

_____

February, 2024

Let the Light in.

TURN YOUR FACE
TOWARD THE SUN

Let the Light in.

Open the windows and breathe in the air
It's time to rise above all despair.

Rejoice in the wonders, enrich your soul
Lean in and listen to the stories untold.

This day, tell yourself a new story, one founded on glimmer and hope
for what's to come for you and future generations.

Turn your face toward the Sun and feel the radiance blaze through
your heart and know the greatest power is the one you hold within to
transform your world. The greatest LOVE is all that you are and the
jewels of Truth are illuminated at this time for those who are willing
to see and Know.

RISE, RISE, RISE! Beyond the illusions lies the greatest revelation of all:

YOU ARE IT - ALL OF IT.

The dark, the Light and colours in between, you are an expression
of Divinity.

———————————————

February, 2024

Every word you speak holds a vibration
creating the tapestry of your life.

THE WORDS YOU SPEAK
HOLD GREAT POWER

The words you speak hold great power, they directly influence your world. Take a mental or conscious note of the words you speak with your natural tongue, then you're encouraged to begin expressing out loud only that which you desire to create.

Practice this consciously for just one day and witness how you feel and what shows up in your experience.

Every word you speak holds a vibration creating the tapestry of your life. Be vigilant with the words you send forth for the magic is in the command and what you believe so shall you create in your world.

March, 2024

God is your provider, your protector,
the gracious giver of all Life.

THE GRACIOUS GIVER
OF ALL LIFE

Ignite the fire of your heart; the divine spark linking you to a limitless supply of vitality, radiance, health and abundance. This is your birthright dear one and those who wish to experience this glory must be willing to strip away - let go - of anything obstructing your link to this Source.

Start your day giving thanks to this infinite supply. Invite it into your experience with utmost faith that it shall be done.

God is your provider, your protector, the gracious giver of all Life. Be in service to God, knowing this approach is the greatest service to yourself - for you can not separate that which you are.

I AM THAT, I AM.

March, 2024

Practice your creative expression as a form of ritual for it brings you closer to God and a state of presence.

CREATIVE EXPRESSION
AS A FORM OF RITUAL

I praise you! I praise you! I praise you on this day for the human experience is host to wondrous creative potential and there are a great many mastering their craft; that which brings you joy. The soul's expression takes form in a myriad of ways and the act of honing a craft elevates your state of mind.

Practice your creative expression as a form of ritual for it brings you closer to God and a state of presence. When one focuses on their craft, the thoughts of yesterday dissolve and your presence connects you to creative energies waiting to co-create with you, to assist in achieving mastery at your craft. Enjoy the process.

March, 2024

*Focus on the beauty, as
simple as this may seem.*

BEAUTY

Devote your focus to presence and gentle care of your mind body and spirit. It is a perplexing time in deed, a web of confusion which is the effect of many losing confidence in their perception of 'normal'. It is crumbling as more are witnessing the absurdity of much taking place in the mainstream and despite this, rather than questioning this troubled state of affairs, many choose to normalise it in their own mind, afraid to dig into the possibility that nothing is as it seems.

Nevertheless, the confusion exists in one's subconscious as they experience further separation from Source and behave in peculiar ways.

It is imperative that one returns to nature to feel grounded, to restore strength and calm. In this state one returns to a deeper connection with Source and faith in the beauty and glory of life on Earth.

Focus on the beauty, as simple as this may seem, for therein lies a remembrance to what's possible for humanity and influences your personal experience of the world you live in.

March, 2024

You are all worthy of love.

LEAN ON ME

This day I bring forth a miracle to those who wish to receive this in the name of Ascended Lord Jesus. As you commemorate this day I step out of the way and shall welcome Him through if you are willing to receive, say:

I AM WILLING TO RECEIVE THE LOVE OF CHRIST.

Accept it done this hour in full power, the glory be to Jesus, who lights up your heart at this time.

Message from Lord Jesus Christ...

YOU ARE ALL WORTHY OF LOVE. GOD DOES NOT DENY ANY OF HIS CHILDREN. KEEP YOUR FAITH IN GOD STEADFAST AND SURRENDER TO HIS WILL AS I DID, FOR SO TOO THIS IS YOUR BIRTHRIGHT AND OPPORTUNITY TO RESURRECT YOUR SOUL AND EXPERIENCE THE ULTIMATE LIBERATION IN THE KINGDOM OF LIGHT. I AM WITH YOU TO HELP GUIDE YOUR WAY FOR THOSE WHO CALL UPON MY ASSISTANCE.

March, 2024

*A wise one knows that good health
is beyond pills and potions.*

LIFE FLOWS IN CYCLES

The stars amidst the infinite galaxy await your precious return. Until then it is imperative that one develops a deeper appreciation of your present experience and as the new unfolds and you step through a portal of new time and space you will begin to feel a whole new world is indeed here.

Life flows in cycles, as does all on planet Earth. And as you align with the natural cycles you will recognise the shifts in your own experience, in contrast to manmade cycles which often have destructive consequences to the mind and body. Your rhythms are nature's rhythms, and her rhythms are your own and the further separated you are from this, the more stress you will exhibit.

A wise One knows that good health is beyond pills and potions. It's connection to God, to the Earth and natures cycles and he who honours the great temple will intuitively discover medicine of the Sacred Heart which heals in radical ways beyond a rational understanding.

April, 2024

The 'other' is also a fragment of 'you' and only love will awaken you to this truth.

UNITY

ALL present on Earth are worthy of this experience; an opportunity to transmute energies into higher frequencies and evolve one's consciousness to BE more like Him. Him is in no religious context, for the energy I speak of is of both masculine and feminine and is not an entity in itself, but the Universal force field of ALL Creation.

There is much fear around the concept of this One Source for there are diverse beliefs on your planet about who and what God is. All perspectives fundamentally have varied degrees of Truth and people are often so caught up declaring their perceptions as just and Holy, disregarding the perceptions of others when they differ.

When you finally arrive at the nature of this Source which is LOVE, you will begin to appreciate and indeed celebrate the diverse expressions of God that you all are and in this appreciation you will REMEMBER the UNITY amongst ALL. For the 'other' is also a fragment of 'you' and only LOVE will awaken you to this truth.

April, 2024

*More discoveries will be made
over the coming years.*

CHANGES TO THE EARTH GRIDS AND SACRED PORTALS

The undercurrents of your landscape are shifting as the collective paradigm is crumbling. There is a rise in consciousness taking place and with it changes to the Earth grids and sacred portals for entry to other realms. These new portals will be discovered by those with an elevated consciousness, who are deemed worthy and entrusted with this wisdom.

They will become the new gatekeepers as they hold a frequency to protect these portals from not just those in the physical, but also the unseen realms.

Yes, indeed there are a great many mysteries and more discoveries will be made over the coming years to assist those on the higher timelines to activate the new way for Earth and all it's living beings. Do not worry yourself with stories of the world for they serve as a distraction from your unique path. Go within for answers and guidance and intuitive insights with who and what to trust. The coming years are unfolding with great uncertainty, for your choices will influence how it all plays out. Every moment, every encounter is an opportunity to activate a higher timeline for yourself and the collective. You are deeply loved and supported even when it all feels helpless, there is always hope. Miracles are your birthright dear one, serve with grace and fortitude.

April, 2024

Step out of the way and stop thinking your way into creating.

BEGIN TO FEEL THE DESIRED OUTCOME

There is no need to wait for anyone to create the change you desire for your experience. Should you have a desire which stems from the love of your heart, this is a call asking to be heard and as YOU embark on creating your desire, the flow of energy supports your will for manifestation to occur.

Many people give up on fulfilling their desires when they don't see results as intended or expect it to take shape in a precise way. The key to manifestation is to allow the natural unfoldment as you take inspired action and flex accordingly.

Step out of the way and stop thinking your way into creating and begin to feel the desired outcome. Play with it, dance with it and rejoice in the possibility, for it already exists in the field. It's ultimately a feeling associated with the desire you are most longing for, more than the form itself. So with this awareness perhaps you can reconsider your approach and spend more time in the feeling to allow the form to take shape in ways you never considered.

April, 2024

There is no separation other than the one you willingly create with your mind.

ONE WITH THE
INFINITE CREATOR

All are One with the infinite Creator and as more continue to expand their consciousness, the stronger this connection is felt. A remembrance that there is no separation other than the one you willingly create with your mind which has been influenced and often controlled by the society from which you are birthed into on this Earth.

Since you are One with the infinite Creator then you are inevitably one with all of creation. The birds, the trees, your family, friends and strangers you meet and everything you define as good or bad.

As more is revealed on your path and your will is to evolve, it requires a commitment to letting go of all you are creating in your mind; the beliefs, the desire to identify, understand, control and return to the central point of focus, the Eternal Now which connects you to the field of One.

May, 2024

Free will is your birthright.

ACT WHILE THE IDEA
IGNITES YOUR FIRE

The brilliance of the Light you shine permeates the galaxies. All beings on Earth have a purpose and no one is left behind, however free will is your birthright. You can radiate the Light of God while incarnate on Earth or choose to dim your Light for fear of what may result.

Many choose to speculate far too long on their ideas and desires and in doing so the momentum diminishes, quite like a flame dwindling. You're encouraged to stop treading so carefully and delight in your ideas; the holiday you seek, the hobby you wish to engage in, the language you desire to learn. Act while the idea ignites your fire and this movement propels energy in the direction, for it is your frequency which impacts the outcome.

May, 2024

*Allow space to commune in solitude with
the parts of you wanting to be seen
and heard.*

GIVE IT ALL UP TO
THE SACRED FIRE

A clearing and cleansing is taking place in the hearts of a great many. Cleansing the remnants of suffering one has held on to for far too long, often spanning lifetimes. This is a time of great transmutation personally and collectively, to help usher in the new. Allow space to commune in solitude with the parts of you wanting to be seen and heard. Send the breath to these spaces, speak to it, acknowledge it. It's safe for you to feel, for the energy is with you to assist the process of renewal. Give it all up to the sacred fire and welcome the freedom which ensues. A lightness and expansion placing you in greater alignment with the path unfolding.

Love is your birthright and the greatest love of all is with the one who stands before you in the mirror, she/ he must learn the greatness within has only just tickled the surface. Life is a joyride when you're willing to embrace all of it with Love.

May, 2024

*To be gentle and strong is
quite a balancing act.*

GENTLENESS IS NOT
A SIGN OF WEAKNESS

Light up the brilliance of this day by bringing your attention to this sweet moment. For that is all there ever is. As you bring your attention to this moment, invite the breath into this space with greater consciousness for it is through the breath you will ease the burdens you keep and dissolve the thoughts of yesterday and tomorrow.

There are a great many stepping forward as the old ways crumble and new paths open for those who have been preparing for this time. Healthy habits and lifestyles will help carry you through, to bare or transcend any challenge.

To be gentle and strong is quite a balancing act. Easier done when you breathe, relax and know you are capable of both. Gentleness is not a sign of weakness, it's an expression of grace, present within all sentient beings. Keep your head up and smile for YOU are the grace and Love of Great Spirit, called upon to express this beauty into the world.

May, 2024

Enter the door of your divinity
through the mantra -
I AM THAT I AM

ENTER THE DOOR OF YOUR DIVINITY

Do not be afraid of the illusions of your mind for they stem from fragments of false conditioning and lose its power when you willingly redirect your focus on Gods power within. If one feels separated from this power, one must take the time to commune with their higher self and meditate without distractions. God's intelligence speaks through the quiet whispers of your soul, the passion and stirrings which activate your divine spark and light you up with vibrance and drive. This doesn't mean you must ambitiously strive for something, but quite simply to experience the vibrance for Life and wondrous experiences the day can bring forth when you take the time to fill your cup through direct communion with your divinity.

There's a spaciousness in the air before the sun rises in the morning, a purity which helps you connect to higher wisdom in your own heart and loving support with you and every soul on this Earth. Speak in the stillness words of appreciation and call forth assistance to allow this support to have a stronger presence in your life. While the possibility is there for intervention in particular instances to assist you, because of free will your request to invite the Love and presence of God and His helpers into any situation brings it forth more rapidly. Or, you can choose to go it 'alone'. But even this is an illusion, for you are never truly alone and your link to Source is within you.

So we encourage you to go within before the sun rises, a time before the noise of the world enters your field and rekindle your connection to your infinite supply. Enter the door of your divinity through the mantra, I AM THAT I AM and give thanks for your experience as it is now in this very moment. Feel the shift elevate you in preparation for the day ahead.

God is your shield and knows the sincerity of your heart and will help you strip away the illusions.

_____

June, 2024

Everything is by design and you are an integral part of the whole.

EVERYTHING IS BY DESIGN

'Let there be Light' ~ words from a well known text, but the true meaning of the command is more than just the concept of creation, but a reference to the forcefield of energy present within all of creation. The old mindset of glory, heaven, Source to be outside of you is a fast fading delusion. Whilst it served a purpose for a period of time to assist with the evolution of human consciousness, the new mindset is being forged and rippling throughout the collective consciousness ~ that you are indeed one with this Light and your unique expression is a dance with Creator. One is not possible without the other and every time you express the glory of this Light in your own unique way, the Light of all creation expands.

Consciousness is ever-evolving and with any growth cycle, there are periods of contraction. You are currently in a period of collective contraction and as one expresses their own Light, it propels growth from within self and others, inevitably leading to a collective expansion into a new era.

It's a masterpiece, it truly is. Everything is by design and you are an integral part of the whole.

June, 2024

You are not your emotions, but your life experience will be affected by the emotions you store.

YOU ARE NOT YOUR EMOTIONS

Freedom follows release. There are a great many holding on to the pain of yesterday without knowing the impact it has on the health of the vessel1. For this vessel to carry you through to better days, it must be frequently liberated of the dense emotion stored energetically.

The resentment, anger, sadness, bitterness, jealousy - all of it is simply energy communicating all the false perceptions you are experiencing toward yourself or another and you can intentionally give it all up to the sacred fire, transmute it with the violet flame or call forth the Light of God to release you from that which is inhibiting your ability to see through the eyes and heart of Love.

It's a wild world out there and the focus is so often on 'out there' without much consideration for 'in here'. What is your vessel communicating to you? For you to anchor the Light of God, for you to express your Love and for you to experience greater peace, you must often release yourself of emotions which disconnect you from this state.

You are not your emotions, but your life experience will be affected by the emotions you store. So, you're asked to frequently listen and release. Apply the techniques; all the tools you've gathered and with loving intentions set yourself free of emotions accumulated from the pain of yesterday.

_____

June, 2024

What entices you to leap out of bed in the morning, if not the glory of another day?

WHAT'S ALIVE IN YOUR HEART?

What's alive in your heart? What entices you to leap out of bed in the morning, if not the glory of another day? Trust in the enthusiasm experienced by ideas and activities as they lead you on a path to elevated states of consciousness and propel you on the path of the higher heart.

Should you take the time to contemplate that which lights you up with joy and enthusiasm and write it down, you will recognise patterns which dance with you from an early age. Self awareness is key to discovering your higher path and it's one which delights the spirit and flows with greater ease and zest for life. Lean in to this, bring your attention and devote time to these experiences and create from this elevated state, dancing to the rhythm of joy.

June, 2024

Only now can lead you to any other experience.

APPRECIATING THE
PRESENT MOMENT

"And you wait..."

Not quite the word people wish to hear. Many on your planet prefer to experience things instantly and your society has been created to enable this at the cost of burdening oneself with obligations to pay back, to owe, to be indebted to something which in many instances was simply fulfilling a sense of dissatisfaction, but the antidote to all dissatisfaction is appreciation.

Your vibration during the period you wait for signs, for guidance for your dreams to set sail influences the manifestation of your desired outcome. So perhaps you consider how the time spent waiting can be better spent – are you focused on what is not present, on feelings of lack, or are you going about your day appreciating what is present and tending to your day-to-day affairs with greater love and care?

What is meant for you is a creation taking form and it cannot be brought to light or realised without patience and a trust in the divine order of all creation, including your own state of consciousness. Appreciating the present moment brings you closer to what is meant for you because only NOW can lead you to any other experience.

_____

July, 2024

Play the drum, listen to the drum beat and let it return you to the Source of One.

SOURCE OF ONE

Reach for the Light of God that dwells within. Go straight to the source of your highest consciousness and it shall draw you up from the ashes and lighten the density surrounding your heart. There are many people on Earth carrying heavy hearts, going about their day believing it to be normal, not even knowing the freedom possible when one invites the grace of God into their day. There are also many at this time helping to transmute the density carried by others, not even aware of their service, not needing to know or prove anything, but simply through their presence and embodying the higher heart, it is done.

You are all connected, your hearts beat as One - play the drum, listen to the drum beat and let it return you to the Source of One.

July, 2024

Lean into your own I AM presence
to show you the way.

ALL HAVE THE
OPPORTUNITY TO ASCEND

There is no distinction between those who have ascended beyond the Earth realm and you, other than your state of consciousness. For all have the opportunity to ascend, to expand their own consciousness in greater union with the Lord God who hath blessed all with the same Light of His source which manifests in form upon Earth. You are a living, breathing expression of source consciousness and so too you have the ability to manifest the Light of God through your physical vessel. Yes, some appear to have less opportunities than others, you have agreed to your path before returning here, but this should not deter you from what's possible for you and your circumstances. You don't need a qualification, a grand home or any other thing, you simply need to believe and honour the kingdom of heaven and legion of Light. Do you choose to repeat the cycles of karma or will you choose in this life now to experience greater soul fulfillment beyond your comprehension?

Your willingness to choose Love, your willingness to have faith, your willingness to lean into your own I AM presence to show you the way and in doing so each day is a courageous act of using your free will for the greater good, your greater good. To create, to play, to rejoice in the great song of Life and dance to the rhythm of your soul, that which knows your time here is temporary and is calling on you to make it count. This day, this breath, be it alone or with the person standing in front of you – let your presence emanate the Light of God. If it your intention, so shall it be done.

July, 2024

Tend to your inner Garden of Eden.

GARDEN OF EDEN

Praise to those who follow their heart in this time of great change. It is upon all souls now to lead with their heart, for it is through the heart and one's union with God that eases the burdens and hardships of the great uprising.

The uprising is here and now within your soul, and you have the opportunity to rise like a phoenix if you are willing to acknowledge all the parts of you seeking a new way, to explore, to create and set yourself free. Diving into the deeper layers and tending to all the bugs, the weeds; the destructive aspects inhibiting your reemergence into a greater light and expression of who you truly are and came here to be.

Tend to your inner Garden of Eden and restore it to its original blueprint, its purity, its beauty and grace. Dig deep and discover the inner treasure, your reunion with the original seed of your creation. As you establish a reconnection you activate a new level of consciousness, one imbued with greater wisdom and determination to remember your own divinity, a force that drives you up through the depths and into a new creation which has been waiting for you all along. Meet it with grace and appreciation. You have arrived.

July, 2024

Consider the larger vision of your life as a masterpiece and each day is an opportunity to build.

YOUR LIFE AS A MASTERPIECE

Bring forth your dreams - the deep stirrings from within that wish to grow through you. There is a need to delight in all that you seek to create. Consider ways to have more fun with the building blocks, the little goals which gradually piece together the larger manifestation.

You and your greater life are a grand manifestation and the fullness or breadth of it comes about through the culmination of experiences. Everything has served a greater purpose for your life now and beyond. The challenges, victories, the skills and resources developed and gained have led to manifestation of the present moment. These have all been building blocks which you've had the opportunity to explore and play with.

So consider the larger vision for your life as a MASTERPIECE - which it is - and each day is an opportunity to build and what better way to build than to play and enjoy the experience.

July, 2024

Trust the natural unfoldment
of your path.

ACCEPT THE NEED
TO SURRENDER

Strive no more, accept the need to surrender. The more you strive the greater the need to force your way through the world. One who learns to let go of everything inhibiting a greater expression of their original blueprint, that which may be considered your 'energetic signature', the easier it becomes to surrender to the essence of your experience and unique path here in this life.

As you awaken to this and have a direct experience of your innate wisdom and power, one loses the desire to strive for anything, for it is given as you move through life dancing the ultimate dance, with the divine. This doesn't mean you sit back and watch the world pass you by, but the inspiration and resources you need to take action, to move, to set the energy in motion awaits you as co-creator.

The path of surrender is a gateway to explore your time on Earth with a more serendipitous approach which doesn't strive it listens, observes and dances with the magic all around. So, sing your praises out loud and rejoice in this grand Creation of life calling on you to trust in the natural unfoldment of your path.

August, 2024

Prayer to reclaim your inner power.

*Holy, Holy, Holy, God our Father,
Come into my heart. Help me to
remember the truth of who I AM;
my power, my freedom, my life force
which flows freely into the beauty and
wonder of this Earthly experience.
Rejoice! Love is here for me now
and forevermore.*

And so it is.

www.ingramcontent.com/pod-product-compliance
Lightning Source LLC
Chambersburg PA
CBHW040747150426
42811CB00059B/1496